Mandala
Coloring Book

Inspire Creativity, Reduce Stress, and Balance
With
30 Mandala Coloring Pages

Vol. 1

Copyright © 2015 V ART.
All rights reserved.

Step Into a World of Colorful Bliss...
Here's How!

Step 1. Gather your tools. Make sure that you have your coloring implements: crayons, coloring pencils, even pens or markers. Don't forget this beautiful coloring book, which is filled with intriguing and intricate designs for you to enjoy.

Step 2. Eliminate all distractions. Turn off that phone, turn off the TV. Make sure your partner and kids know that tonight you're spending quality time with yourself! Find a quiet spot where you won't be disturbed and get ready to relax.

Step 3. Start coloring! You can color your pictures with wild abandon, or gently and carefully. Do what feels right for you. And remember, there are no wrong colors to use, or wrong ways to apply and combine them. If you make a mistake, that's OK -- it's really just going to enhance the beauty and originality of your chosen design.

Step 4. Color to your heart's content. Enjoy this respite from your busy day. Just immerse yourself in this creative and fun pastime and forget your worries. Unleash your inner child, and revl in memories of simpler times as you make something beautiful.

Step 5. When it's time for you to finish, no problem -- simply stop coloring and put everything away. Remember to put your tools somewhere handy so that you can come back and enjoy this book whenever you need some relaxation. Also, do not feel compelled to finish your picture in one session. If you're not done, no problem: leave the rest for next time.

Step 6. For extreme fun and long-term stress management, repeat these steps often!

5 Great Ways to Use This Awesome Book

This book is great for fun, meditation, and also for color therapy.

1. You can't do it wrong- You can only do it right!
That is great, isn't it? The designs you will find in this book are made so that you can color them, you can go about this however you like it, you can color inside the lines, or outside the lines, you can also do both, whatever gives you pleasure. You have the choice of choosing whichever pattern or color that you like.
I will also like to inform you that you can use this book for meditation. Here's how:
a. you can select any mandala that calls or attracts you.
b. make your choice of colors, those colors should be those that resonates well with the pattern you have chosen.
c. with joy, begin to color the paper, just flow with it and fill the spaces on each page with color, lines, dots and shapes. You can even use words!
 d. Flow with the process! Don't get disconnected.

2. Masculine style mandala coloring
 This is an active search for the point of wholeness, of nothingness. Immerse yourself into those patterns, let the noise that's all around you and creating that turmoil fade away, focus on each of the stroke you are making, you will be released as soon as you complete coloring and you will feel refreshed, I guarantee you that.

3. Feminine style mandala coloring
There is an abundance of joy in the world, you've got to find it. This style is a celebration of the abundance of joy. Fill your vision with color. Take pleasure in the caress of your pen. Your fulfillment will be in the process.

4. Make it about someone else
This is very interesting, remember that life is not all about yourself. you can also make this journey about someone else, it will benefit you a great deal. For example: you can choose an important figure to you- like your mother, or father.

Go about coloring it mindfully, as you reflect on every characteristic of such relationship. You will find forgiveness, compassion and understanding. You may even discover a way to celebrate such important relationship. Now, can you just imagine what a blessing that would be? It would be just great.

5. Color therapy

This is also of great advantage for those who need 'color therapy' this book is a very useful tool for color therapy. If a specific chakra requires energy, you have the liberty to select its' color and fill the entire mandala with shades and values of that color.

Now, remember to keep the mandala at a place where it would be very much visible to you, this will help you to focus more on the energies you want to nurture.

Most importantly, mandalas are a wonderful way to enjoy color and quiet doodling for pleasure.

Here is a warning for you: Beware, they are addictive!

www.ingramcontent.com/pod-product-compliance
Lightning Source LLC
Chambersburg PA
CBHW080545190526
45169CB00007B/2646